EPISTROPHY

TED PEARSON

DOS MADRES

2025

DOS MADRES PRESS INC.
P.O. Box 294, Loveland, Ohio 45140
www.dosmadres.com   editor@dosmadres.com

Dos Madres is dedicated to the belief that the small press is essential to the vitality of contemporary literature as a carrier of the new voice, as well as the older, sometimes forgotten voices of the past. And in an ever more virtual world, to the creation of fine books pleasing to the eye and hand.

Dos Madres is named in honor of Vera Murphy and Libbie Hughes, the "Dos Madres" whose contributions have made this press possible.

Dos Madres Press, Inc. is an Ohio Not For Profit Corporation and a 501 (c) (3) qualified public charity. Contributions are tax deductible.

Executive Editor: Robert J. Murphy

Illustration & Book Design: Elizabeth H. Murphy
www.illusionstudios.net

Typeset in Adobe Calibri & MadisonSquare
ISBN 978-1-962847-41-4
Library of Congress Control Number: 2025948302

for Stephen Emerson

"Modernity is the transitory, the fugitive,
the contingent, which make up one half of art, the other
being the eternal and the immutable."

– Charles Baudelaire

EPISTROPHY

1

Memory of the future is fading fast.
This is the so-called end of history.

The gift of life is the search for meaning,
not the presumption that meaning exists.

Madness traces a familiar silhouette.
It's never too late to be where you are.

Perfect symmetry unmasks a vacancy.
Locals call it "the pit of despair."

Bad omens tell of a world in transition.
As velocity picks up, time slows down.

2

Critics disdain what escapes them,
resulting in death by interpretation.

Language and thought arise together.
Home is a speck on a pale blue dot.

Narrative seems an invasive species.
Its endings intend us to beg for more.

Indelible phrases gloss what have you.
Radical particulars define an era.

Ambiguity colors the inessential self,
which leads to a politics of grammar.

3

Where up for grabs is down the alley,
second thoughts are risk averse.

The past is immured in former glories,
while the present has yet to find itself.

Do trees dream of becoming forests?
Can mutual aid be extended to all?

Between conception and dissolution,
the organism resembles a flame.

"Done and dusted" was Earth's epitaph,
whence our nostalgia for the future.

4

Gnarled allusions stumped some trees.
The poem at large contains multitudes.

We are but buskers on history's stage
whose weary vocables aspire to music.

Nimble fingers articulate grace notes.
Any subject would seem an indulgence.

He finished his work before nodding out.
The life of letters was truly demanding.

Then came thoughts of inexistence as
the peace that surpasses understanding.

5

Lyrics issue from a sultry chanteuse
with every whispered syllable intact.

A spotlight pierces the moonless night.
Everything changes. *Nothing* ever does.

A conundrum as quiet as death itself.
Where the only solution is dissolution,

your scars are emblems of a difficult past,
but are not predictive of your future.

Time passes slowly on a clock without
hands. Eternity smiles in approval.

6

Consequent to finding each other,
we form communities of practice.

Hunting and gathering words where
we find them, only to end in perdition,

the familial home of accursed poets
and last port-of-call for fallen angels.

The planetary refuge for the human
project, which has made of it a hell.

Blood at the root of our dark histories
stains the pages of the lies they tell.

7

Music is a mode of organized sound.
Poetry translates words into words.

Mournful echoes rise in the distance,
bereft of the peace that silence brings.

From the wire in the blood to the wire
in the rose, a sea-change decades

in the making. The poet observed that
writing is hell and words are unforgiving.

Much like the dead, which is why, on
reflection, he chose to write for the living.

8

Drifting in a dream through a desert
town, under a tent of stars. In which

the disambiguated subject appears,
somewhat the worse for wear. The long

night tempers the golden dawn to
which he woke in wonder. They are

sad companions, who now are ghosts,
whose mordant whispers fill his head.

There to grace his work with words
they've culled from the silent dead.

9

Migratory music followed the tides.
Modernity signaled a change of key

(while innovations in typography
followed in its wake). Even where

sound and sense held sway, tradition
favored the "perjured eye." Ideology,

then, as a specular phenomenon, in
which we recognize ourselves. That's

when we burned the map we'd followed
from birth, only to end up here.

10

I know where *I* belongs, and it's not
exactly heaven. What, after all, makes

pronouns personal if not the people
who use them? The regime neither

speaks with nor listens to reason.
And we, who would wake from our

decades-long slumber, must accept
that we don't matter to the cosmos.

To whose sublimity we can attest,
and the fact that it's not heaven.

11

There's no escaping the violence of
nature. Belief that the cosmos exists

for some purpose gives rise to fervent
superstitions. In part, it's a question

of credulity and an endgame some find
unthinkable. But, at least as far as

we know, contingency allows for few
absolutes. Hence, we live for desire, not

duty. Seeking words from anywhere that
speech is illumined by truth and beauty.

12

No spirit haunts the remains of culture.
Where pockets of human reason persist,

they dismiss the religionists' accounts of
cataclysm. Their only sin was being born.

Most survivors were stunned by nature's
indifference to their self-inflicted wounds.

While those who yearned for the rapture
found it. And then, in lieu of the human

arts, turned to their silent god for comfort
and to do their thinking for them.

13

Are not the undulations of deep and
shallow sleep akin to those of thought?

Great depths can only be inferred from
the distant echoes of their rumblings.

Both are essential to sleep and thought.
But the raised surface is the work site

where our inferences are made. These,
by convention, we call poems. They are

signs of what's at stake when thought
resounds with sounds like music makes.

14

Does our temperament shape our thought?
How, indeed, could it not? We are but

the distillate of lived experience. That
includes the life of the mind, which

colors our temperament over time and
thereby shades our thinking. In age,

as our losses outweigh our gains, we
turn to the blues to ease our pain.

Then, with the courage born of struggle,
we turn to face our fate, unblinking.

15

All manifestos are aspirational. This
accounts for their rhetorical excess.

Invariably, once someone "sees the
light," they are blind forever after to

the darkness within. The voice that
once cried out in the wilderness had

no discernible effect. Thus chastened,
the prophet returned with lowered

expectations. Much like those to whom
he preached on self determination.

16

Imagine a painting without fixed
dimensions, neither point, nor line,

nor plane. Under gallery lighting,
you can clearly see no pigment colors

the canvas. No shapes are drawn in.
No objects or strings are attached.

And, no clues identify the artist, who,
for reasons known only to himself,

never signs his paintings, or reads
reviews, or ever attends an opening.

17

In what tense do your memories occur?
In what sense are some events said to be

truly memorable? As texts harbor subtexts,
images rehearse what's been lost to us

over time. What do we presume to read in
these faces, now beyond recall? For some

of us, *names* are talismanic, more than any
image. Conjuring comrades from times past

to stand with us in the perilous present
that was the future we once had shared.

18

Nothing that exists is exempt from change.
History will date the voice, the gesture,

the notion, and the deed. All point to
our liberation from whatever falsehood

would claim us. Thus, as we read be-
tween the lines – if only legible to few –

a veritable trove of possibilities appears.
As Heidegger says, "there is a clearing."

That is the focus of our present thoughts
and the site of our final words.

19

It was always a choice, to dwell amid
the ruins, or to clear them away and

build anew. History's exclusions are
cautionary tales. They are cryptonyms

for traumas that haunt the broken
world, the only world we know.

Approaching the end of this grand
experiment, we can only wonder at

our undead past, the toxic present,
and a future that doesn't include us.

20

So many sutures, so little time. Thus,
the quotidian makes its demands, and

we record some intermittent music in
what stolen moments we can manage.

Indeed, we're common thieves of time,
although from here it looks more like

we're taking back our own. If the bosses
can pay for the busywork we do, then I

see no reason that they can't pay us for
keeping the language free and true.

21

The poet was bound to show up
because he has skin in the game.

Even if it's the skin of his teeth
by which he hangs suspended

above the Void of inexistence,
otherwise known as his study.

There he pours over cognitive
maps, which is how he views his

poems: fragments of the periplus
that will one day guide him home.

22

Hope well knows it will end in defeat,
but you can't play the language game

without it. It's the game, not the out-
come, that matters. Its endless innings

cut short by death, which is the final
defeat. In lieu of which, you struggle

with the everyday language of desire.
That which wants what it wants when

it wants it. Hoping, even as you near
the end, that there's still more to come.

23

The text foregrounds the message to
invoke the poetic function. Its source

is no less than the low-ghost himself.
He, who bares his teeth to falsehood,

is thrillingly alive to the beauty and
transformative power of language.

Even as poems aspire to poetry, poets
aspire to fail ever better. The rubric

says to handle each word with care,
lest they be lost to the dissembling air.

24

What makes simplicity hard to attain?
When is it ever as simple as it seems?

For any body (of works and days) in-
volved in the aftermath of our tragic

genealogy, a certain *ressentiment* obtains.
No one ever asked to be born, much less

born belated with a millennial mess to
clean up. Yet, we cling to existence. And,

"when difference is raised to its highest
power, the first affirmation is *becoming*."

25

With wisdom comes grief as time expands
for the man of constant sorrow. Between

new abstractions that give him pause and
old urgencies that hurry him along, he sets

a measured pace, disdaining the low-hanging
truths he passes on his way to the foot of

Parnassus. Where begins the arduous climb
that he faithfully makes each day – hoping,

as he approaches the summit, that in time
the locals will invite him to stay.

26

The untranslatable kernel of the poem
is a black hole within its verbal fabric.

Nothing escapes its fatal purview.
It absorbs and processes all before it.

Politics revolves around what is
obvious and how to leverage it;

the unspeakable echoes the totality of
existence. And it's our fate to speak it.

In the end, the intrepid poem quickens
as it enters the event horizon.

27

When life fails to appear as a miracle,
it comes to resemble a curse. Having

exhausted his appetites, the subject
approaches a state of detachment,

in which life is neither *here* nor *there*.
Not so much a matter of indifference

as a sense of insurmountable loss.
First, the years that are lost to time.

Then, the fact of a failing body that
would take a miracle to revive.

28

Art gives hope to those who attend it.
Not because it *offers* hope, but because

it knows hope sustains our practice,
whose only attainment is failure.

So says the song of reality as sung by
a chorus of failures. Whose lyrics

extol the art of poverty and whose only
motive is to see another sunrise.

In which light, the poet admits that
the simplest things are hardest to learn.

29

You don't ever want to come between
a martyr and the author of his death.

Who stamps the coins, rules the land.
Who burns the flag is a headline.

And if nothing changes, nothing
happens in the bleak episteme of

the moment. Meanwhile, the people
have called for a referendum on death.

A telling measure, if one were needed,
of how far they've drifted from reality.

30

Because watching someone stare
at a wall is boring beyond belief,

we invented the lives of the poets.
To survive one's passion is to be

abject. Creation evolves in a fertile
Void. Inertia provides false access

to eternity. Dead poets will be just
as dead when they're "discovered"

a lifetime later. Living poets want
for readers while they are still alive.

31

Translating thought into the language
of the senses links the reality of art to

the people. Not as an ideality, but as
a purely practical matter. In this way,

aesthetics underwrites politics, seen
in the broadest of terms. Because you

can't act on what you can't see, and
that makes change impossible. Hence,

these tableaux that make it plain that
our pain is both palpable and political.

32

Who seek democracy seek the traces
that suggest it remains a possibility.

First, to describe the human as *the set
of all possible humans*. And then,

to embrace the assertion of rights that
advance the human project and *not*

dominion over others. Poetry begins
with the refusal to know one's place.

It maps out the backroads to elsewhere.
And at present, democracy is elsewhere.

33

Poetry stages a "logical revolt" against
any regime (aesthetic or political) that

shutters reality in favor of its delusions.
Delusions rooted in the psychopathology

of present-day cognitive capitalism.
When the elders went to the mountain

to die, they made their peace with the
living before they left for the summit.

There they made their peace with
death and welcomed the end of pain.

34

To the grammar of probability we
prefer that of desire. Desire which is

imbricated in every work we write.
Thus, the search for "gratified desire"

that fires the imagination, the seat of
our cognitive exploits. And death?

How does that enter the discourse?
As a process, a becoming, and an end

in itself. Which, not unlike desire,
comprises a community of bodies.

35

Poems may take many paths, but all
point to the one destination, regard-

less of the poet's intentions. A poem
can take no other path than the one

laid out by its constant evolution within
the reality that surrounds it. There

is a disorderly dynamism in life that sub-
tends the mathematical sublime, that

which scales up to include the cosmos
and the silent music of the spheres.

36

A true gift exceeds what justice requires.
Consider the gift of undying love, which

embraces that which others are content
to judge and dismiss out of hand. It is

the apotheosis of the human bond,
though cynics view it as bondage. Such

is the outcome of love gone wrong, which
tempers our desire with pure negativity.

Loved or not, we presently recall and
relive a past that we can't forget.

37

As waves are water's advance guard,
the surf is the contact zone between

sea and land. Between the restless and
the seemingly stolid. Between every

instance of language (the waves) and the
domain of language as such (the sea).

Thus, the import of human language
is that it makes us human. We, whose

transports stem from our encounters
with language, thought, and reality.

38

We tend to forget that we're *all* self-
fashioning. And that social life is

a masquerade. Of course, we're not
what they say we are. But we're also

not who we think we are. Hence,
the impulse to see *through* the subject

leads to a richer discourse. One that's
beyond the imagined limitations of

your no less imaginary self. The one
now living what remains of your life.

39

Why should your public-facing mask
have to satisfy others' expectations?

Especially when convention amounts
to pleasing others at your own expense.

They want your compliance, not your
multiplicity, the very thing they sought

to conform to their hegemonic values.
Values they've been preaching since

the day you were born. A day that in
time you might come to regret.

40

Language is the medium in which we
dwell, and syntax is the basis for our

comic attempts at coherence and for
contact with each other. Given that

language changes us as we change it
in turn. When I was young, flaneurs

were my heroes, though some found
them absurd. So one praises the poète

maudit – his allegiance to modernity
and the power of the written word.

41

Diminished expectations are de rigueur
for those whose faith in language has

also been diminished. Those who ignore
what the written word has to offer.

Poets are poets in any kind of weather.
They reverse engineer the anxiety for

closure to reclaim what was once thought
possible. This enlivens the realm of desire,

which fosters, in turn, our recurring
dreams of arriving anywhere but here.

42

Musician of silence and endless night.
Whose hyperboles we never spoke of.

Whose ecstasies lay hidden under guilt.
And whose vision of impossible figures

recalled the onset of creation. His work
trafficked in words. Not ideas. And he,

like Moses, led his tribe toward a future
he would never see. His tragic flaw was

his dismissal of the flesh, even as he drew
his symbols from ads in fashion magazines.

43

It's curious how many poets say
that they'd rather play music or paint.

But why say it if they don't mean it?
Do they fear our gift for failure?

Regardless of what we make of the
results, there's a long tradition of

painters and musicians who were
fearless when attempting poetry.

They knew well the tactile pleasure
of working with fresh material.

44

The numbers are large, but the math
is simple. There's plenty of food for

everyone. The problem resides in its
distribution. There's a dearth of

compassion, a lack of political will.
It's clear that food should not be

weaponized, but that's precisely what
the hegemon has done. Where food

is a commodity and not a right, the
poet notes that "people are starving."

45

The question was, what does it mean
to arrive? When critical success meets

popular demand, the results might be
canonical. Sans demand, and known

to few, the poet writes for friends and
strangers and to see what's on his mind.

Thus, he has thrived without a career,
even though he's never arrived.

That is so because he's never found
a compelling reason to leave.

46

Realism is what we see according to
how we see it. It's not reality per se.

Far from being alone in the universe,
we're connected to it by the stellar

debris of which we all are made. And
which lends us a cosmic pedigree.

Realism as representation is one way
of thinking through life as we find it.

By asserting our objective existence,
we become lifelong seekers after truth.

47

Golden light through the window at
sunrise. No dreams lurk to despoil

the day with longing or regret. I see
the unhoused wandering like ghosts

on the streets where we played as
children. I watch the lines at the food

bank growing longer by the day.
I can only hope (against all hope)

for my struggling neighbors nothing
less than the little I hope for myself.

48

Physics proposes that a single
molecule from your larynx can

instantly affect a molecule inside
a star at the edge of the universe.

Thus, we're entangled in the fabric
of space-time and thereby connected

with the rapidly expanding totality
of existence – at least to the extent

we can grasp it. And, in this way, if no
other, we are far from being alone.

49

Behind every order is a great disorder.
Framed beneath a vault of blue,

it's ironic how the survivors number
their remaining days with primes. Quick

studies, if short lived. Unlike the time-
less chaos to which they will return.

Chaos, then, is the contact zone between
the Void and the gradual emergence of

a new cosmic order (each time inclusive
of a bit more chaos than the last).

50

"Continue," said Kierkegaard, "I'll
discover where you sweat." Which

describes a normal day in the life of
the poet. Sweat beads his brow at

every caesura. Fear at the thought of
missing a beat when fire brings light

as well as heat. Considering all that
remains to be done, he has no

choice but to carry on and trust
the poem will survive the flames.

51

Your actual existence is objective.
Your experience of it is not. All of

a sudden, the woodwinds trilled,
breaking cover in the white land-

scape. Burnished echoes streamed
from the Void. Strictly old school,

rich and sonorous. You have had
good reason to fear the unknown.

Despite your years of stoic resolve,
you're still afraid of dying alone.

52

Down at the crossroads, a parting of
ways. The farewell you so carefully

crafted forever stuck in your throat.
So, we shared a wordless embrace,

more telling than a thousand pictures.
A waning crescent scarred the sky

as it had the night we met. It's easy to
remember, if impossible to forget.

Down at the crossroads, as if by design,
we were as one for one last time.

53

Memory conjures the ghosts of our
elders, who are now disinterested

observers, and not the people that
we once knew. They're not here to

judge us, but "to witness and adjust"
to existence beyond the world they

left behind. But, before we can join
them in perpetuity, we must lay our

fear of dying aside. Once they take
your ticket, it's time to take a ride.

54

No progression without contraries,
measured in units of resistance.

Once the changes grew overly familiar,
players started phoning in their solos.

Hard-pressed to stay employable, heavy
backbeats grew heavier still. Meanwhile,

the youth market burgeoned and swept
up hard-earned entertainment dollars.

The tradition has long since recovered its
luster, but never regained its mass appeal.

55

Lyn says, "The obvious analogy is with
music." At once a provocation and an

inspiration. As was indeed her wont.
But, be it sonics or phonics, nothing

is audible without an atmosphere.
The interminable silence of space must

envy our tendency to break into song.
And what is song but words and music

united for the nonce? A subtle art that
flourished long ago in old Provence.

56

Shade tempers the noonday sun, but
nothing tempers your out-of-body pain.

Those who choose to ignore bad history
are those who will make much more of it.

And just when you think you've seen
it all, you see it all again. Diminished

expectations grow ever more diminished.
Hence, your dreams are all the same, and

every dream repeats its theme: you
"don't get around much anymore."

57

Modernism started with a throw of
the dice and will end when the fog

of war burns off. Right reason steers
clear of gaming and war, though

neither is alien to human nature.
Nor is the decision to write poetry.

Whose appeal is its alterity, which
affirms our love of otherness. A quirk

that may make us strange to others
and certainly other to ourselves.

58

The band's new single, "My Chimera,"
is riding high on the charts. It seems

to have struck a chord in its listeners'
imaginary. Much like a handshake is

a sign that you're unarmed, we shield
ourselves from presumptive definition.

The chimera's evolution from myth
to delusion marked a signal advance.

But, delusions aside, the fact remains
we have reason to believe in monsters.

59

How discern the music in the noise
that phonemes make? The haptic taps

that conjure words and breath that bids
them speak? Aristotle placed courage

first above all other virtues. He says that
without it, those virtues are impossible.

Even as these poems anticipate disaster,
they echo everything we've ever heard.

Then, they blend those diverse voices
in a message made entirely of words.

60

Through-composed music, unlike the
plastic arts, required the invention of

written notation, as did the literary arts.
But, there's a difference in arranging

phonemes and sonemes to produce
their respective texts. The difference

is the absence of language in music,
except in the lyrics of songs. Where

"words," according to Mozart, "must
be the obedient daughters of music."

61

Memories of the future are fading fast.
Our critics disdain what escapes them.

Where up for grabs is down the alley,
gnarled allusions stumped some trees.

Lyrics issue from a sultry chanteuse,
a musical form of biological bonding.

As song is a mode of organized sound,
migratory music follows the tides.

In dreams begin new possibilities. Which
is how I know exactly where I belongs.

62

There's no escaping the violence of nature.
No spirit graces the remains of culture.

Undulations vary between deep and shallow.
Does one's temperament shape one's thought?

All manifestos are essentially aspirational.
How else imagine a picture sans dimensions?

In what tense do your memories occur?
Nothing that exists is exempt from change.

It was always a choice to dwell amid ruins,
with so many sutures and so little time.

63

The poet showed up with skin in the game.
Hope well knows it will end in defeat.

The text foregrounds the message to invoke
what makes simplicity hard to attain.

With wisdom comes grief as time expands
the untranslatable kernel of the poem.

When life no longer seems miraculous,
art seeks those who choose to engage.

You don't ever want to come between
the poet and his thousand-yard stare.

64

To return the word *liberation to* language,
who seek democracy must find its traces.

Poetry stages a "logical revolt" against
the endless flurry of tyrannical edicts.

Poems may indeed take many paths, but
a true gift exceeds what justice requires.

Waves are the ocean's advance guard.
Don't forget, we are *all* self-fashioning.

But, why should your public-facing mask
hide away the multitudes within you?

65

Diminished expectations are de rigueur
for the poet of silence and endless night.

The population of poets has since exploded.
The numbers are large, but the math is simple.

The question is, what does it mean to arrive?
Where realism traces how we see what we see,

string theory posits that vibrating strings
are the primary stuff of the multiverse.

Behind cosmic order lies a great disorder,
where chaos searches for its missing parts.

66

Even as your actual existence is objective,
down at the crossroads, a parting of ways.

To conjure is to remember and recall
there is no progression without contraries.

While "the obvious analogy is with music,"
the question remains. *What* is analogous?

Modernism started with a throw of the dice.
The band's new album is "My Chimera."

How discern the message from the noise
which is the ambient music of the streets?

67

As velocity increases, time slows down,
which leads to a politics of grammar.

"Done and dusted" is idiomatic for
the peace that passes understanding.

Time passes slowly on a clock without hands.
There's blood at the root of our dark histories.

On principle, we only write for the living –
words we've culled from the silent dead.

We play on the changes that led us here
after paradise proved to be lost.

68

Our collective pain is palpably political.
At present, democracy is elsewhere.

In time, we'll make our peace with death,
which in turn makes communities of bodies.

There's music to which we will not dance.
A mishmash of wishes, lies, and dreams.

Emotion recollected revivifies the past
you shared with friends now gone.

On a day that you might well live to regret,
you demand concessions from the universe.

69

A waning crescent scarred the star-crossed
night. Your fear of dying alone is real.

In death, we join the disinterested dead,
whose status has gained some posthumous luster.

With his words and music in seamless array,
the old man creates a final playlist. What

makes us unique makes us other to ourselves.
We have good reason to believe in monsters.

Where our last best words anticipate disaster,
in their absence, impossible music thrives.

70

To treat the poet for melancholy
is like treating water for wetness.

It wasn't precisely happiness that
we promised one another, but rather

the adventure of a lifetime together.
In the end, an epistemic adventure.

For which there will be no grand
finale. It's not that kind of thing.

But, if you want to make him smile,
be kind and bid the poet sing.

ABOUT THE AUTHOR

TED PEARSON was born and raised on the San Francisco peninsula, a seventh generation Californian. After early musical training, he began writing poetry in 1964, and subsequently attended Vandercook College of Music, Foothill College, and San Francisco State University. In 1976, he published his first book, *The Grit* and began his long association with the San Francisco Language Poets. He has since published over thirty books of poetry. He coauthored *The Grand Piano*, a ten-volume experiment in collective autobiography. He edited a posthumous edition of Craig Watson's last poems, *Epilogue*. And he co-edited *Bobweaving Detroit: The Selected Poems of Murray Jackson*. His essays have appeared at intervals since 1975. He lives in Northampton, Massachusetts.